Praise for *SMART Living*

"*SMART Living* arms you with the knowledge and confidence to approach, interact, and build trust with others."

—Joseph Grenny, Co-author of the *New York Times* bestsellers *Influencer, Crucial Conversations,* and *Crucial Confrontations*

"An enjoyable ride—*SMART Living* is packed with unique and valuable ideas."

—Rich Feller
Professor and President, National Career Development Association

"Hard-hitting ideas in an easy-to-read and entertaining format."

—Richard Paul Evans
#1 New York Times bestselling author of *The Christmas Box* and *The Walk*

"*SMART Living* will change how you think. It puts the power in your hands. It is the re-examine, re-charge, re-create guide that will lift your sights and your spirit."

—Darby Checketts
Author of *Customer Astonishment: 10 Secrets to World-Class Customer Care*

"John's SMART living principles helped me with the motivation and sales strategies to get the first key customers signed for my consulting start-up. There is no down economy if you implement the strategies in this book."

—Mitch Brinton
Principal, Virtual CMO Consulting

"John Boyd's approach is world class. We have benefited on a daily basis from the SMART living system that he developed."

—Alan Davidson
CEO, Customer Elite

"John's straightforward, focused approach helped me land the exact job I carved out. I actually enjoyed the process. I do not fear losing my job knowing if I had to, I could do it again."

—Rhett Barney

"*SMART Living* is full of the principles and concepts we all need. From helping its readers change from a W-2 to a business perspective, to the amazing illustrations to help its audience capture and internalize its message, this book is a must read."

—Ken Kaufman
Founder and CEO, CFOwise, Bestselling Author, *Impact Your Business*

"John's principles for seeking an optimum life have played a significant role in shaping my career path. His ideas helped me land my first full-time sales job in financial services out of college. I increased my salary a year later by 228% using John's free agency philosophy. This carried over into my entrepreneurial ventures—resulting in the founding and sale of three technology start-ups."

—Chad Fullmer

The Illustrated Guide to SMART Living

The Illustrated Guide to

SMART

Custom Design Your Life

John Boyd

Illustrated by
Mike Bohman

Tremendous Life Books
118 West Allen Street
Mechanicsburg, PA 17055
www.TremendousLifeBooks.com
www.facebook.com/TremendousLifeBooks
www.twitter.com/TraceyCJones

The Illustrated Guide to SMART Living: Custom Design Your Life

Tremendous Life Books titles may be purchased for business or promotional use or for special sales. Please contact Tremendous Life Books for more information.

Book Design by Paul Killpack, Highland, Utah

ISBN 978-1-936354-31-3

To my Mother,

who has the courage of a thousand lions.

Acknowledgements

I started working on this book about seven years ago and completely gave up on it twice. I have many people to thank for helping me to make it a reality. Karen, my wife and friend for the past twenty years was my head coach, editor, and cheerleader throughout the process. She spent endless hours helping me to untangle my thoughts and get them into coherent written form. This is partly her book.

Mike Bohman created all of the illustrations. With his amazing talent and vision, the concepts have come to life. Paul Killpack did a fantastic job on the design of the book cover and interior. His clean and elegant style captured my intent perfectly.

I'm grateful for the editors of Precision Editing Group, as well as Laurie Cisneros for helping me to express myself in a readable way. Karen Christoffersen of BookWise Publishing lent me her legendary book production talent and gave me the coaching and encouragement I needed to finish the project. Thanks to Meagen Bunten and Dian Thomas, as well as the BookWise authors, for giving me energy and motivation.

Alan Davidson helped me to crystallize many of the ideas in these pages and his encouragement and editing contribution have been critical. Thanks to Kris Boyd, my brother and business partner, for his insight and coaching. I'm grateful to my father, who has been my lifelong sales, business, and personal mentor.

Celesta Davis is the prototypical autonomous agent—she has customized her career on her terms. Her editing input was invaluable. Thanks to Chad Fullmer and Brad Jensen for their influence on my approach to career management over the years. My children have also played a pivotal role in this book—they inspire me to be a better person.

Table of Contents

SMART – Move

SMART – Attract

SMART – Relax

SMART – Test

Introduction

Josh makes $120,000 a year and hates his job. He's a talented programmer who sits in a cubicle ten hours a day writing code. He is expected to account for his time in 15-minute increments and he feels like someone is always looking over his shoulder. He loves creating software, but his lack of control over how he spends his day makes him resentful. When he talks about his job, his frustration is obvious. He feels trapped.

Research has shown that we have a basic psychological need to feel as though our actions are freely chosen. In other words, emotional health depends upon ongoing feelings of autonomy. Autonomy means that our activities and goals are self-determined and are in line with our interests and values.

The lack of this self-determination is a strong predictor of negative emotions, such as frustration, helplessness or hopelessness. Having little control over our day can be a significant source of discontent.

Throughout my career, I have tried to create a life where my activities are largely self-chosen and are aligned with my interests and values. The resulting lifestyle has contributed greatly to a sense of personal happiness and freedom.

The process of successfully customizing my own career has sparked a desire to help others create a life that gives them greater feelings of autonomy and fulfillment. My goal is to assist you in defining and creating the life you want.

The first section of this book will challenge you to redefine how you think of yourself and your process for goal achievement. The remaining five sections will take you through my SMART goal achievement model.

Included in the concepts are instructions for taking action toward your goals, as well as ideas for avoiding obstacles that might stop you from moving toward the changes you desire.

Each concept is associated with a full-page illustration, and many include a story. All of the stories are true, though some of the names have been changed. These images and anecdotes add clarity to the concepts. Hopefully, the ideas in the following pages will motivate you to take chances, make changes, and custom design your life.

All truly wise thoughts have been thought already, thousands of times; but to make them truly ours, we must think them over again honestly, until they take firm root in our personal experience.

—Goethe

The biggest mistake that you can make is to believe that you are working for somebody else. Job security is gone. The driving force of a career must come from the individual. Remember: Jobs are owned by the company, you own your career!

—Earl Nightingale

Autonomous Agent

I want to ask you to think in a way that may require a subtle, yet pivotal shift from your current perspective. Think of yourself as a unique, autonomous agent who has the ability to clearly define your ideal life and the confidence to make it happen.

Why? Because you must believe that you have the power to choose your life experiences before you will be able to take control. If you do not believe you have some control, you are unlikely to make a change, even if you desire it.

Being an agent of your life means taking personal responsibility for those choices. Instead of passively accepting your circumstances, you use your autonomy to actively seek the changes you desire.

If you have the mindset of an autonomous agent, you are in a position to proactively create your ideal life. Whether you are an employee or a business owner, a stay-at-home mom or a football coach, perceiving yourself this way will give you power to achieve your goals.

See if these concepts inspire you to a more independent way of thinking about yourself...

The great and glorious masterpiece of man is to know how to live to purpose.
—Michel de Montaigne

Cog in the Machine

Throughout history, people worked in small towns or villages as independent farmers, shopkeepers, and blacksmiths, etc. Resourcefulness and ingenuity, combined with hard work, made people productive and successful.

With industrialization, corporations began to dominate many of the world's economies. Time clocks, policy manuals, and managed processes began to diminish individual initiative.

Instead of being small, autonomous entities, individuals became dependent, generic components of the corporate structure. As a result, workers began to feel like their identity was absorbed by the corporation and that their individual efforts had little impact on the company's production or progress. They became cogs in a corporate machine.

Many feel the same today.

I want my identity back. I don't want to be known as the CEO of AOL Time Warner . . . I'm my own person. I have strong moral convictions. I'm not just a suit. I want poetry back in my life.

—Gerald Levine

Back to the Farm

Fortunately, changes in information technology are making it easier for us, as individuals, to take more control of our lives. Activities can be done at any time, in any location.

A graphic designer in Chicago can work on a project for a client in London. An American exchange student in China can make sales calls for his uncle in Los Angeles.

We're returning to our more entrepreneurial, pre–Industrial mindset. Most of us aren't farmers or tradespeople, but we can think and act like them. We can treat our lives as they did.

More than ever, you have the ability to be the architect of your life if you embrace and utilize your autonomy. Like a small farm or business, you are in control of whether you work hard and succeed, or stagnate and fail.

Accept that the responsibility of accomplishing satisfying goals lies with you personally. Use your creativity and ingenuity to create a unique product—You—that you can sell to the world.

If you don't design your own life plan, chances are you'll fall into someone else's plan. And guess what they have planned for you? Not much.

—Jim Rohn

Cubicle Captivity

Maybe you've been laid off and cannot find a job. Or you're working, but aren't making enough to pay the bills. Or you're engaged in activities that aren't completely fulfilling. Perhaps you have a nagging urge to do something more with your life.

If so, you are in cubicle captivity. You feel trapped and have little hope. Captivity is miserable. If you stay in a situation like this for long, your happiness and motivation will decrease.

> *Jason was working as a language translator about ten years ago. He was making $15 an hour and was bored with his job. He was also in the process of declaring bankruptcy because of an investment that went south. Though he knew he could do better, he didn't have a college degree and felt like his options were limited.*

It's easy to feel like Jason, even if your circumstances are different. When you don't like your current situation, and you don't know how to make a change, feelings of discouragement can be overwhelming.

If you want total security, go to prison. There you're fed, clothed, given medical care and so on. The only thing lacking . . . is freedom.
—Dwight D. Eisenhower

The Great Escape

There is a way out. You have the ability to escape the captive mindset and gain more control. The first step is to believe that you can create a satisfying life.

> *Jason resolved to take the initiative and make a change. As he left his bankruptcy attorney's office one day, he decided to walk into a technology company across the hall and ask about software development opportunities. He was told by the hiring manager that an opening for a Java programmer would be available in about a month.*
>
> *Despite his lack of programming experience and formal education, Jason took some risk upon himself and offered to do the job without pay until the opening was confirmed. They agreed. He learned enough Java in that month to keep the job and successfully launched a career that today allows him to consistently earn a six-figure income while doing work that is challenging and enjoyable.*

Jason believed in himself and confidently approached the company. He took a calculated risk and creatively closed the deal. Even if your escape from the captive mindset isn't exactly like Jason's, don't be afraid to be creative and move forward. Begin to consider possibilities that might give you a chance at a "Great Escape."

One can never consent to creep when one feels the impulse to soar.
—Helen Keller

My Great Escape

The next step in escaping cubicle captivity is to clearly define your goals. Do you want more flexibility, more money or more control? Do you want more training or different responsibilities? Do you want to work for someone else or work for yourself ?

I experienced my most recent "Great Escape" when I decided to start my own sales consulting company. Though I had enjoyed my sales jobs, there were a few things over which I wanted more control. I wanted to travel less and have more time to spend with my family. I also wanted to create several sources of income by working with multiple companies, instead of being an employee for one business.

Using my sales expertise, I focused primarily on generating revenue and improving sales performance for technology companies. I made a few phone calls and soon I had my first client. I felt like a cubicle refugee.

Today, I continue to maintain contracts with several clients. My independent business has allowed me to more fully achieve my personal and professional goals—including the creation of this book.

As you identify your life preferences and define your goals, you will be better able to make progress. The more clearly you define them, as specifically as you can and preferably in writing, the easier it will be to achieve them.

The secret to happiness is freedom, the secret to freedom is courage.

—Thucydides

Think Like a Self-Contained Business

Do you think like an entrepreneur? It's a subtle, yet important distinction. You have the power to dictate how to market, sell, and deliver your services regardless of whether you are an employee, an independent contractor or a business owner.

Employee Mindset	Business Owner Mindset
An employee relinquishes most of her control to an employer, giving up initiative in her work.	A business owner feels ownership in her work and treats her employer like a customer.
An employee mindlessly punches in and out on a clock until an unemployment crisis occurs.	A business owner is always marketing and networking so she is ready to find new opportunities when needed.
An employee takes company policies, including compensation structure, at face value and doesn't consider negotiating.	A business owner questions everything and negotiates to get the most mutually beneficial situation possible.
An employee does a good enough job not to get fired.	A business owner takes pride in her work and continually increases the quality of her services to the customer.
An employee feels dependent on the employer for her future.	A business owner knows her value stems from her productivity. She keeps her skills current and her value high so she is ready for the future.
An employee holds tightly to her job and paycheck, fearful that others will take them away.	A business owner perceives others as collaborators who will help to grow her opportunities.

Sculpt Your Career

Hopefully, the chart in the previous section challenges you to consider how you think of yourself. Do you feel like you can negotiate with your employer? Do you assume the job you have now is the first of many opportunities? Or do you feel like you are stuck in your current situation?

As you proceed through the rest of the book, please keep in mind this image of the woman sculpting herself. She represents the ability you have to "chisel out" the person you dream of being.

Of course, different adversities give each of us a unique starting point and may slow the process. For instance, you may have to work at less-than-desirable jobs while putting yourself through school. You may have a disability or illness to consider as you chip away at gaining valuable work experience. It may take longer than you think, and it may be harder than you expect.

But whatever your circumstances, I am certain that right now there is a goal to set, a choice to make, or an action to take that will lead you toward a better, more desirable life.

As you learn to think like an "autonomous agent," eventually you will find that you have more choices and that you can custom-design your life. The people I have worked with who have persevered in their quest will confirm that the outcome is well worth the effort.

Everybody's a self-made man; but only the successful ones are ever willing to admit it.

—Anonymous

Daniel Pink's Declaration of Independence:

When in the course of economic events, it becomes manifest that traditional work arrangements stifle innovation, reward timidity, devolve into nothingness, and offer at best a perilous prosperity, it becomes necessary for citizens of conscience and talent to break free from that decaying tradition and declare their independence.

And so we, the working women and men of America, declare ourselves free agents—and declare these truths to be self-evident:

Who we are and what we do should not stand on opposite sides of a psychological divide. So for us, work is personal! We are committed to unifying our personal interests and our business interests, our lifestyles and our work styles—because we fundamentally believe that we will be happier and more productive if we work and live as whole people.

Nothing is permanent. Security is an illusion. A work life based on workplace insecurity is no work life at all. So we choose the freedom to be ourselves and to follow our interests. And we are discovering that, in an economy of opportunity, freedom promotes security. The more we work in our own best interests, the more secure we become.

As free agents, we are choosing our own work paths—choosing the clients we want to work with and the projects we want to work on. And we are distinguishing ourselves from our colleagues in the old workplace by reserving the right to say no! No to clients who are hard to work with, who underpay us, who ask for proposal after proposal (but never hire us).

We've spent too much of our working lives running scared—scared that we'll be laid off, yelled at, or blamed for something that wasn't our fault. And what have we learned? That fear doesn't motivate us for long; eventually it impedes our performance. Top performers become great by playing in their own terror-free zone.

—Daniel Pink, *Free Agent Nation*

Notes:

SMART Living

Stand Out from the Crowd

Once you have an autonomous-agent mindset, you can move forward and find the life that is right for you. In the following pages, I have outlined a sales model that I call SMART Living.

The SMART concepts are divided into five sections: *Speak, Move, Attract, Relax,* and *Test. Speak* is about how to find and connect with other people. *Move* covers the importance of managing risk and consistently taking action. *Attract* discusses how to increase your value and create demand for your services. *Relax* shares ideas for eliminating worry and stress as you work toward your goals. And finally, *Test* teaches you how to validate your assumptions, and negotiate your terms.

As you read through these principles, do your best to apply them to your own unique situation. Your specific personality will determine which ones will be easy for you, and which ones may require more effort. However, I am confident that by consistently utilizing these concepts, you will set yourself apart and increase your ability to achieve your goals.

SMART – Speak

The Magic of Human Interaction

Consistently speak with as many people as possible about your thoughts and goals. Something magical happens when you get out and talk to people about the changes you desire. New relationships and new ideas will arise that will help you in your efforts.

How does this happen? Conversation can be a powerful learning experience. As ideas and questions are exchanged and processed, participants think of things that they didn't know or understand before.

Speak to people about what you are doing, what you want to be doing, and how you hope to accomplish your goals. More importantly, ask about what other people are doing in their lives and how they are achieving their goals. As you engage with friends and colleagues, you will gather valuable information that will help you refine and adjust your goals.

For most of us, creating these kinds of interactions can be difficult. Talking to others about personal goals is often intimidating. This section will guide you to see how essential these connections are to your success and increase your confidence to create them.

Communication—the human connection—is the key to personal and career success.

—Paul J. Meyer

The Human Connection Flash Point

When I begin an interaction with someone, I watch for the moment that a bond is formed. If it happens, it's usually after we have had some meaningful dialogue. At a particular moment, we connect on a personal level and an unspoken alliance is formed.

> *One day a prospective customer joined me for lunch. At a certain point in our conversation, he apparently felt enough trust to tell me about some problems he had been having at work. We spent most of our lunch talking about his situation and brainstorming ideas that might help him.*
>
> *By the end of the meeting I noticed that the nature of our relationship had changed significantly. We went from being business acquaintances to friends intent on helping each other. I became a confidant for him, and he became an ally for me, helping me to close a $200,000 sale. Each of us had a new perspective about the other, underwritten by the trust of having shared personal challenges and deliberating with one another about solutions.*

Once this flash point of trust occurs, the relationship changes; both parties become intent on helping each other achieve their goals.

The meeting of two personalities is like the contact of two chemical substances: if there is any reaction, both are transformed.

—C.G. Jung

Cut Through the Noise

The most important element in goal achievement is consistent action, and the most important action is direct contact with others. Peoples' minds are distracted by everything from sales quotas to their bad golf game. Direct contact is the quickest and most efficient way to break through this distraction, get their attention, and uncover new opportunities.

When I was sixteen, I bought an old truck that wouldn't start unless I put a few drops of fuel directly onto the carburetor. Making a call directly into a targeted company is like putting fuel right on the carburetor—it tends to start the engine right up.

You may be reluctant to make direct contact. It might seem easier to pursue more indirect methods for moving your goals forward. For example, for job seekers, responding to ads and sending out resumes is not as intimidating as calling a person directly.

However, pursuing job ads has a very low rate of success. Most opportunities (approximately eighty percent) are filled before they are even advertised. Your efforts to connect with prospects will be more immediate and more productive if you contact companies and initiate interviews yourself.

When I am coaching, I often make cold calls with job seekers to demonstrate the process. On one occasion (and this happens often), the first manager that I called was at that time looking for someone to hire. If it can happen in the first call for me, it can happen in the first call for you.

Make Direct Contact

I recommend the following steps for making direct contact:

1. ***Research*** desirable companies and find specific people by using the Internet. Fill in any information gaps by calling the company and asking questions.

2. ***Make a list*** of your ten favorites. Learn more about what they do, their profitability and growth, who makes decisions, etc.

3. ***Call each contact*** on your list and take notes of the results. Make at least ten new calls each day.

4. ***Filter your list*** as you get new information and continue to refresh the list by repeating steps 1, 2, and 3.

When I finished my MBA, I targeted a specific technology start-up for my first job. I found the number for the CEO, called him directly, and told him I'd love to sell for him. He said that I had to wait until the new VP of Sales reported for work because he would be making those hiring decisions and was moving from Silicon Valley shortly.

A couple of weeks later, I found the VP's new home number and called him there before his first day of work. I introduced myself and we talked about how I could help him. A month later I was his first hire. We've been close friends ever since.

To succeed in sales, simply talk to lots of people every day. And here's what's exciting– there are lots of people!

—Jim Rohn

Make Your 10-Second Pitch

Once you get someone on the phone, what do you do? Most people are on information overload. You will have about ten seconds to capture his attention. Be ready with a short, powerful message. Here is a sample script divided into five steps:

1. ***Introduction:*** "Hi, my name is John Boyd. I'm a software engineer focusing on Java and PHP."
2. ***Respect:*** "Is this a good time or should I try back later?"
3. ***Pitch:*** "I've been a programmer for the past eight years with companies like X, Y, and Z, and I think I might be able to contribute to your company."
4. ***Setup for the invitation:*** "If you want to compare notes sometime, I thought perhaps in the next week or so we might have a short chat."
5. ***Invitation for a phone or office meeting:*** "Would that work for you?"

Plan out your pitch in writing and be comfortable with the flow of the conversation. Rehearse different tones until you find your confident, relaxed voice. Then make your calls. Once you get someone hooked with your 10-second pitch, you can set an appointment for a deeper discussion.

Though you should have a basic plan, don't worry too much about what to say. *The act of calling is much more important than your technique.* As you make the calls, your technique will gradually improve.

After you've made your ten or so calls for the day—regardless of the results—take a break. Eventually, consistent daily action will pay off.

Manage and Multiply Your Connections

Developing and nurturing strong connections with both friends and contacts is an important resource. If you are willing to reach out and develop new relationships, you will open the door for more work opportunities to come your way.

The people with whom you already associate comprise your existing network. Start by emailing at least twenty of these contacts, asking for their help. Explain that you are looking for new ideas and leads.

More importantly, continue adding new contacts to your network to strengthen it and make it a more valuable resource in your job search. You may want to:

- Take colleagues and prospects to lunch and get to know them better.
- Attend relevant trade shows and industry events and actively introduce yourself.
- Connect contacts with common interests to each other.

Recently, my friend Kevin went to a networking event sponsored by a local business group. He was skeptical that it would be a productive use of time. However, while there, he began talking to a young man whose father-in-law happened to be a prominent investor in the area. From that connection, Kevin was able to meet with the investor and discuss a potential investment opportunity for his business.

The time you spend developing relationships with others is a valuable investment. I have witnessed repeatedly how small, consistent efforts to nurture these connections eventually pay off.

Get People Out of the Office

There is something unique about the relaxation and bonding that occurs when people eat and socialize together outside of the office. Trust can develop when you have an opportunity to personally interact with another individual. These conversations can develop a depth in the relationship that phone and office visits alone usually do not.

A few years ago, I made a last-minute trip to Montreal, Canada to visit a potential customer who had traveled to attend a trade show. Over a two-day period, we ate meals together and attended several of the trade show events. It changed our relationship. We had a great time and I knew a friendship was developing. Soon after the trip, despite robust competition, he chose to buy from my company.

Because I made an effort to get to know him outside of the office, our business relationship became a friendly, mutually beneficial one that has lasted for years.

Lunches and other face-to-face activities provide you with opportunities to build trust in your relationships. In these more casual settings, your interactions with others can be transformed into deeper, more meaningful connections.

Internalize the Golden Rule of sales that says: All things being equal, people will do business with, and refer business to, those people they know, like, and trust.

—Bob Burg

Questions are the Fuel for Building Trust

Asking good questions and listening to the answers is the discovery process by which you find common ground and begin to establish trust.

Thoughtful, relevant questions open people up to discussion and dialogue. Questions create opportunities for needs and feelings to be shared, in addition to facts.

As you ask questions, find opportunities to ask deeper questions which may lead to more meaningful dialogue. Here are some examples of starter questions that can lead to trust-building interactions:

- Where are you from?
- How long have you lived in this city?
- Where did you go to school and what did you study?
- What do you like to do in your free time?
- How long have you worked here? In what capacities?
- What are some of your current business challenges?
- How does that impact you and the company?
- What are your career goals beyond your current job?

If you are not accustomed to asking questions like these when you are networking or interviewing—practice. Find chances to get to know someone better by using one or more of these examples. You will be amazed at the connection you are able to create.

12345

Use Self-Interest to Your Advantage

> *I was recently selling my services to a technology company in a competitive situation. My competitor was in the conference room with the prospects while I waited for my turn.*
>
> *After he left, I sat down with the three buying managers and without slides or brochures, I started asking questions about their current situation. What was working for them and what wasn't? What problems were they actively trying to solve?*
>
> *For over an hour, I continued asking questions about their business and listening to their answers. I understood what they needed, and they knew it. Then I was able to share with them how I could assist their company.*

How was I perceived in comparison to my competitor? One of the managers unexpectedly called me during my drive home to offer me the contract—specifically, he said, because I had spent the time in our meeting learning about their business needs. Instead of focusing on myself, I focused on their problems and where they needed help. And this immediately built trust with them.

When in an interview or similar situation, remember—it's all about them. Ask questions until you understand their needs. I guarantee you will capture their attention and spark their curiosity.

You can have anything you want in life if you can help enough other people get what they want.

—Zig Ziglar

Show Your Cards

Have you ever been in a conversation with someone who mentions goofing up on a project or admits to saying something stupid in a meeting?

What impact would this kind of honesty have on you? Would you feel like you knew that person a little better? Would you be more willing to let your own guard down?

As an example, sometimes I tell this story to my clients.

> *I was selling a software product to the Canadian Postal Service, based in Ottawa. Due to my hasty travel planning, I flew to Toronto instead. Luckily, I was able to catch a quick flight to Ottawa, making me about thirty minutes late to the meeting.*
>
> *Then I had technical difficulties during my presentation. Needless to say, it was a lackluster performance. A few months later, I won the deal, but the prospect said that it was in spite of me that they chose us. The product carried the day.*

I like to share this story because I want them to know that I am comfortable showing some of my vulnerability. It invites others to bond with me in a more intimate way.

When interacting with others, you may be afraid to reveal any weakness. However, not being genuine makes it harder for them to connect with you. No connection means no trust.

Speak to others about yourself and your situation sincerely. People will be both surprised and reassured by your openness and will likely respond with more openness and trust themselves.

SMART – Move

Maintain Consistent Activity

> *In the TV miniseries Band of Brothers, there is an intense battle scene where a lieutenant is immobilized by indecision just as he begins a dangerous attack on a German stronghold. He is paralyzed by fear, leaving his troops exposed to enemy fire and compromising the mission. Remarkably, another officer rushes into the middle of the fight to replace the incapacitated officer and continue the attack.*
>
> *Realizing that he must communicate with a second squad of soldiers on the other side of the battlefield, the new officer charges directly into the line of fire and breaks through the enemy line. He gives his men their orders, and runs back to his original position. So unexpected was his exploit that the German troops were stunned into inaction. They literally sat and watched as he penetrated their ranks—twice!*

Moral of the story: *Taking action is more important in goal achievement than anything else. Action is more influential than technique, tactics, talent, pedigree, or intelligence.*

The more action we take, the more information we get. And the more information we get, the better we are able to improve what we do. In other words, consistent daily action helps us make smarter decisions.

Move. Act. Stir up some dust. Try something new. Then try something else. Opportunities will come as you take action.

Stake Your Claim

A few years ago, I strategized with Steve who wanted to fly for a large regional airline. He had obtained his pilot's license several years prior, but had only been flying cargo carriers part-time. He wasn't making enough money, he was bored, and he was in a rut.

It was time for him to "stake his claim." Together we began to outline his action plan. For the first time, he wrote down his intention. Just that first act—writing it down—shifted not only his attitude from defeat to hope, but his perspective from impossible to achievable.

At the airport a few weeks later, he saw a group of employees wearing the uniform of his desired airline. With his new mindset, he gathered his courage, walked up to the group, and began asking them questions about the company. Could they offer him any advice on getting hired?

Coincidentally, one member of the group happened to be the VP of flight operations for the company. A few days later, Steve received an interview packet. He was hired shortly thereafter, and six years later he is still happily employed there.

Decide. Plant a stake in the ground declaring who you are and how you will serve others, even if your plan isn't perfect. Begin by writing down your goals as clearly as possible. Your goals give you a starting point from which you can begin your search.

Take Risks

Try new things and reach out to people in new ways.

It's possible to become paralyzed by fear when you think of doing something new or uncomfortable. To overcome your fear, look honestly at the real costs of a choice before deciding what action to take. Usually the downside is not as bad as you imagine it.

One way to measure the actual risk of an action is to imagine what could happen in the worst-case scenario. For instance, you are afraid to call someone to ask about their needs. Cold calling is new to you and you just aren't sure what to say. What is the real risk? You mess up the conversation and hang up the phone. Your ego gets hurt—but you might learn something too.

If the real risks are too great, think creatively about ways to reduce them. For example, if I am working out a contract with a client, and he wants to commit me to a longer time frame than I'm comfortable with, I propose a ninety–day trial period. Instead of over-committing myself or losing the deal, I lessen my risk by suggesting an option that works for both of us.

Have the courage to fearlessly assess risk. Do not miss an opportunity because of an unknown, unmeasured risk. Calculate it, manage it, and then proceed with your plan.

And the day came when the risk to remain tight in a bud was more painful than the risk it took to blossom.

—Anaïs Nin

Give Ego a Time-Out

Ego, or how we think of ourselves, often gets in the way of desired results. Here are three of the most common, most paralyzing ego risks.

- **Rejection.** You might be stopped in your tracks because you don't want to hear "no." All sales efforts carry the risk of being turned down. Practice hearing it and moving on. Rejection cannot hurt you unless you let it stop you.
- **Embarrassment.** You might not be qualified. You might not know what to say. You might say something wrong. These feel like risky situations. But what do you have to lose? A little ego and one attempt at success. If you make a mistake, you'll know what to do better the next time. Do not let this stop you from acting.
- **Failure.** No one likes to try something difficult and then get no results, or end up further behind. Failure can help you improve if you don't let it discourage you.

Give your ego a time-out. You will be more willing to take risks which will help you move closer to your goal. In addition, when others sense that your ego is in check, you will be able to build more trust with them.

Confidence comes not from always being right but from not fearing to be wrong.

—Peter T. McIntyre

E

Failure by Default

As you work toward your goals, you may begin to doubt that you can ever achieve them. You may be tempted to take yourself out of the game.

You might stop networking or pursuing desired opportunities. You might quit following through on inspired thoughts and ideas.

> *Richard Paul Evans tells a story about taking himself out of the game. In high school, he dreamed for months about asking out a particularly beautiful girl. She sat right next to him in one of his classes and he resolved to take her to the homecoming dance.*
>
> *But each time he tried to ask, his fear took over, and he chickened out. Sadly, she went to homecoming with someone else. At a reunion years later, after both were married to other people, she asked Richard why he had never asked her out. She had had a crush on him all along!*

Richard had failed by default. He eliminated himself from success when he let assumptions and risk control his choice. He assumed her answer would be no. Fearing the ensuing rejection and failure, he quit before he even had the chance to succeed.

Avoid selling yourself short by giving up too early in the process. Let others tell you "no"—do not do it for them.

Defeat is not the worst of failures. Not to have tried is the true failure.

—George Edward Woodberry

Playing It Too Safe

We all know the saying, "If at first you don't succeed . . ." But the reality is that failure hurts. And most of us will avoid repeating painful experiences if we have a choice.

I've watched several of my clients push their efforts intensively for a while, and then when something goes wrong they give up. Even worse, I've seen them return to a job or a pay level that they planned to leave behind because their disappointments were too stressful. After failing in their first few attempts at improving their situation, they decided it was either too hard or not worth the stress.

It's easy to lose your motivation as you pursue your goals if you've suffered feelings of defeat. Indeed, doubts about your ability to succeed may even compound your stress.

Persistence through the pain of failure is a key to changing your life and achieving your goals. Whenever you experience a failure, you are getting critical feedback. All of your efforts—whether they yield positive or negative results—create valuable experience. And the information inherent in that experience directs your next decision and action.

Eventually, you will make progress. And those successes will outweigh the failures. Don't let yourself "play it too safe." Expect that you will be able to make the changes you desire. Then continue taking action toward your goal, even as you experience both failure and success.

Learned Helplessness

Dr. Martin Seligman conducted a groundbreaking experiment in which he administered shocks to dogs who were placed in boxes from which they could not escape. Next, he put the same dogs into open boxes that they could easily exit. But when shocked, they did not try to escape or even attempt to avoid the shocks. Dr. Seligman named this concept "learned helplessness."

Does this principle apply to you? Have you experienced so many rejections or failures that you have given up trying to succeed?

When you feel completely discouraged, it's easy to slip into a stagnant, despondent state. Often, your despondence stems from negative thoughts which become exaggerated over time. The thoughts turn into debilitating messages that your mind repeats over and over, detailing your weaknesses and the hopelessness of reaching your goals.

Dr. Seligman recommends aggressively challenging these persuasive thoughts —actually arguing with them. A negative message may tell you that no one will want what you have to offer because the economy is down. Argue the opposite—that companies always appreciate good value and you just have to find the right opportunity.

If you try, but cannot overcome learned helplessness by yourself, don't suffer unnecessarily. Seek help from someone you trust, like a good friend or therapist, until you start feeling better.

People often say that motivation doesn't last. Well, neither does bathing—that's why we recommend it daily.

—Zig Ziglar

Mud Bog

Much of the discussion in this section has been about the ways you can get stuck as you pursue your goals. You become afraid of the risks. You quit taking action because of failure and discouragement. You go back to the status quo because it's familiar and safe, even if you hate it.

When you feel yourself being hindered by any of these issues, take some kind of action to counter their effect. The key is to create and maintain momentum.

Here are some activities to get you moving again:

- Talk with someone who inspires you and can help give you new ideas or energy.
- Refresh your target list.
- Send email to your connections.
- Go knock on a target company's door.
- Write in a journal. Writing untangles thoughts.
- Pray or meditate to clear your mind.
- Do something kind for someone else. Service creates positive energy.

Similar to your life depending on oxygen, your success depends on momentum. Do something each day that moves you toward your goal.

Achievement seems to be connected with action. Successful men and women keep moving.

—Conrad Hilton

Changing Trains

As you experiment with various goals, sometimes you may find yourself going in the wrong direction. This situation will require a major change, which can be difficult.

It's tempting to stay in a given direction longer than you should. Sometimes you may be tempted to persist even when you know it's time to move. Other times it is fear that may hold you back from making a big change.

Early in my career, I took a position with a modest base salary plus commission. After six months of hard work, I realized that this opportunity was moving much too slowly for me, and I would not be able to achieve my income goal by the date I had planned.

A colleague opened up another opportunity in a more mature market with a much better compensation plan. With my income objective in mind, I jumped at it and met my goal that year.

As difficult as major course corrections can be, find the courage to recognize that your current situation is no longer taking you in your desired direction. Set a new goal and start looking for new opportunities.

There are costs and risks to a program of action, but they are far less than the long-range risks and costs of comfortable inaction.

—John F. Kennedy

Diversify Your Portfolio

Investment professionals like to say that the best way to protect yourself against losing your investment is to diversify your portfolio and spread your risk. Here are three ways to reduce your risk.

1. **Create multiple sources of income if it makes sense for you.** For example, I contract with different companies at the same time for my consulting services. If I lose one customer, I am still making money with the others.

   A computer programmer might have a full-time day job, but moonlights smaller contracts in his free time. A dental hygienist may work on different days for two different dentists. Multiple clients keep a career flexible and ensure that income stays consistent.

2. **Diversify your skills.** Of course, you will want to balance the need to specialize with the desire to diversify. A software programmer may learn a new computer language to improve his skill set. An insurance salesperson might add life insurance to broaden her services.

3. **Diversify your network.** If you have only been keeping in touch with family and friends, start attending network events in your specialty. Use Internet resources to connect with other professionals. Having a broad, diverse group of contacts will help protect you from long periods of unemployment.

SMART - Attract

Attract, Don't Persuade

My son once asked me how I persuade people when selling to them. He said he didn't think he would be able to do that. I told him that when you are selling, you are not doing something *to* someone. Instead, you *attract* them to your product by providing them with what they want, when they want it.

> *I have a friend who is an expert fly fisherman. He's in constant motion, checking the time, looking under rocks to determine fly types, and finding the perfect bend in the river where the fish might be hiding. When he casts into the water, he manipulates the line so that it looks as natural as possible, drifting down the current. He knows he must attract the fish with his bait. He cannot force it to bite.*

When you sell yourself, you are offering your unique "bait"—your particular blend of talent and skills. You must be valuable to your prospects to attract their interest.

Your attractiveness and value in the marketplace will grow as you build a base of expert knowledge. You cannot force this attraction. Instead, it develops from a solid foundation of expertise, based on your skills and experience.

Success is not to be pursued; it is to be attracted by the person we become.

—Jim Rohn

Become a Proud Craftsman

Becoming an expert at anything is a long-term commitment. People go to school for years and encounter numerous situations in life to gain the skills and experience they need to become excellent.

> *Will Smith, the only actor to star in eight consecutive films grossing over $100 million, once said that you have to "beat on your craft" continually by working harder than anyone else to become an expert in your chosen field.*

Most successful people will tell you that it took them longer and required more energy than they expected to achieve their goals. Be prepared to commit your best efforts and a lot of your time to gain the skills and experience you will need to succeed.

How do you determine if you are pursuing the right craft for you? Here are a few indicators:

- You are infused with energy.
- You become unaware of time/appetite.
- The work seems easy and effortless.
- You feel peaceful and happy while working.
- People compliment your ability.

A positive psychologist, Mihaly Csikszentmihalyi, coined the term "flow" to describe this state. When you are perfectly challenged and perfectly interested, your experiences become fun. Seek for chances to experiment until you experience "flow." Your value will increase as you become a proud craftsman.

Catch the Vision of Your Potential

Most of us start our lives without a clear vision of what we want to become. As you accumulate knowledge and experience, you will begin to have greater clarity about the kind of goals you want to accomplish. This vision will enable you to better articulate your goals to others.

If you currently feel unsure about your strengths, consider these ideas for increasing understanding of your interests and potential:

- Take personality or interest tests. Career placement centers and online resources offer many of the most popular assessments. Though not definitive, these tests can be a helpful first step.
- Accumulate education and experience, seeking specifically for "flow" experiences.
- Ask for and accept feedback from people you trust.
- Use inspiration and intuition.

Not only is knowledge of your abilities essential for setting goals, it is also essential for attracting the marketplace. Seek for a better understanding and awareness of what you have to offer, and you will be better able to attract an opportunity that is right for you.

Continuous effort—not strength or intelligence—is the key to unlocking our potential.

—Winston Churchill

Expert Knowledge Creates High Value

The only way to become attractive and consequently more valuable to the market is to have expert knowledge.

> *In 2008, the University of Utah football team was undefeated and ranked number two nationally. For Head Coach Kyle Whittingham, his years of experience finally paid off and his value as a coach skyrocketed. To keep him from accepting another position, the school doubled his salary from $600,000 to $1.2 million!*

For most, it takes years to get to the expertise level of Coach Whittingham. However, high value is available to anyone willing to spend the time and energy required to gain the necessary skills and experience. Here is the cycle:

Skills and experience lead to expertise. Expertise increases value, which strengthens leverage in the market and creates more opportunities and choices. Value, leverage, and opportunities continue to grow as this pattern cycles over time, which gives you a greater ability to achieve your goals.

High Value Creates More Leverage

As you accumulate more value from your increasing expertise, you'll have more leverage in the marketplace because there will be greater demand for your services.

> *Deion Sanders was one of the greatest cornerbacks ever to play football. He could close the gap between a football and a receiver better than anyone, resulting in an amazing career record of fifty-two pass interceptions.*
>
> *In 1995, several premier teams courted his services, causing the "Deion Sweepstakes," as it was called in the media. Sanders signed a contract with the Dallas Cowboys ($35 million for seven years and a $13 million signing bonus), making him the highest-paid defensive player in the NFL up to that time.*

Sanders was attractive to the market because he built an expertise in a very specialized, highly-paid niche. As his skills and consequent value grew, demand for his work increased, which strengthened his leverage.

Like Sanders, raising your value gives you greater power to choose your terms. You will have more "muscle" to determine how, when, where, and at what price you will offer your services. This hard-earned leverage empowers you with more choices and more opportunities to develop.

Find a meaningful need and fill it better than anyone else.

—Anonymous

High Value Creates More Choices

The high value/high leverage correlation leads to more choices in two significant ways.

First, more opportunities become available to grow your expertise when you are valuable to the market. The best scholarships, contracts, and jobs go to the most valuable candidates.

For instance, because of your value, a highly satisfied client may recommend your services to a colleague, enabling you to increase your income.

Second, high value/high leverage gives you increased power to choose how to accomplish your goals. Maybe you want to maintain your current income, but work half the hours.

Or you may wish to become better at what you do so that you increase your annual earnings. You may want to travel, or you may prefer to work from home.

What would you choose? Whatever you desire, if you have high value, you will be better able to control your personal situation and assert your preferences.

High Value Leads to More Confidence

The more value you have, the more confident you will be. Use that confidence to help in achieving your goals.

> *Karen approached me at an industry trade show wearing a homemade tag around her neck that read, "#1 Salesperson." I was a VP of Sales for a technology company and was not looking for a salesperson at the time. However, I ultimately hired her anyway because I saw that she could help me achieve my sales goals for that company.*

She staked her claim on being a must-hire, valuable salesperson and had the courage to act on her assertion. The self-confidence she exuded immediately grabbed my attention. I hired her not only because of her qualifications, but also because her confidence made her value more attractive to me.

Some of the benefits of self-confidence are:

- Self-assured demeanor
- Poised tone of voice
- Relaxed facial expressions
- Initiative to ask meaningful questions
- Courage to negotiate personal preferences
- Consistent networking and prospecting
- Selectiveness in choosing work opportunities

Continually Increase Your Value

If attractiveness in the marketplace is dependent upon value, you will want to keep your value high, which is an ongoing process. Take advantage of every opportunity to improve your knowledge and experience so that your value will continue to rise.

What are some of your favorite activities for boosting your value? Reading books, researching online, or taking classes can increase your knowledge base.

Experimenting with new processes or strategies, talking to mentors, and volunteering can help broaden your experience and give you new ideas to implement into your current situation.

Whatever you decide to do, commit yourself to learning new skills or trying new ideas on a regular basis. Continue building your expertise and the market will reward you accordingly.

Personal development is your springboard to personal excellence. Ongoing, continuous, non-stop personal development literally assures you that there is no limit to what you can accomplish.

—Brian Tracy

Resist the Box

Others may try to decide for you what you should do and how you should do it. Whether innocently or intentionally, they may try to put you into a box of their own expectations, regardless of your best interests.

Pressure to conform to these expectations may come from employers, customers, colleagues or friends.

I have had clients who wanted me to work in their office or change my pricing because it was easier or more convenient for them. I am always willing to assert my preferences while clearly and reasonably proving my value to them.

Maybe you get an offer that is significantly lower than what you are worth. You feel pressure to accept the offer even though you know you are worth more.

If your market value is high, you will have enough leverage to negotiate your preferred terms or continue looking for alternate opportunities.

To be nobody but yourself, in a world which is doing its best, night and day, to make you everybody else—means to fight the hardest battle which any human being can fight; and never stop fighting.

—E.E. Cummings

Base Your Pricing on the Impact of Your Contribution

> *Once upon a time there was a beautiful ship with a broken-down engine. None of the owners or their mechanics could fix the ship, try as they might. Finally, they brought in an old man who carried a small tool bag. He looked the engine over carefully, from top to bottom. Then he reached into his bag, pulled out a little hammer, and gently tapped something. The engine roared to life!*
>
> *But when the bill for ten thousand dollars came, the owners were incensed. The old man had hardly done anything. So they wrote the old man a note saying, "Please send us an itemized bill." The man sent a bill that read: "Tapping with a hammer: $2. Knowing where to tap: $9998."*
>
> *—Islamic Legend*

As you gain value and leverage in the marketplace, you will have a greater ability to negotiate the level of your compensation. Like the old man, you will be able to base your pricing on the impact of your contribution.

Start by identifying your unique contribution. For example, if you are good at closing deals, you will increase their revenue. If you are good at hiring and managing people, you will keep morale and productivity high. Then be courageous enough to ask for what you are worth and get compensated well for the value you offer.

Maximize Income Per Hour

The profitability of annual salaries can be misleading because salaries alone fail to account for the quantity of hours required to earn them. Many people who thought they were making good money are shocked when they calculate their actual hourly wage.

> *Kimberly was making about $150,000 annually working seventy hours per week; her hourly rate was about forty-two dollars per hour. She began adjusting how and where she worked, and managing her time and travel better until she was working fewer hours while keeping her earnings steady. By reducing her weekly hours to around forty, she raised her hourly rate to seventy-five dollars per hour, nearly doubling her hourly earnings.*

How can you maximize your income per hour? Here are some ideas:

- Do not undervalue or undercharge for your level of expertise; keep your rates high, commensurate with your market value.
- Improve your delivery of services so that there is no wasted time, i.e. work from home instead of in the office, travel only when necessary, minimize meeting time, etc.
- Hire others to relieve you of easier work, like administrative tasks, preparation and set-up tasks, etc.
- Add more clients to increase overall cash flow.
- Make sure your time is focused on activities that are aligned with your personal and professional goals.

If you are currently paid by salary, make sure to quantify how much you actually earn per hour. Then find ways to maximize your hourly wage so that you can better meet your goals.

SMART - Relax

You're Not in a Hurry

Well, okay, you may feel like you are in a hurry. Lack of progress in your goal achievement can be disheartening. However, the process of improving yourself cannot be rushed. It takes effort, time, and patience.

If you pursue an option and there isn't a fit, be enthusiastic about moving on. Do not become too attached to any particular opportunity. Getting a "no" is okay. Saying "no" is also okay. You don't want to force a decision and end up with in a situation that is no better or even worse than your current one.

Relaxing allows for two important things to happen. First, you will be less stressed and exude a more confident demeanor. Second, you will not act desperately, which will give you more credibility as you interact with others.

It may take longer than you would hope. You may have disappointments and uncertainties. Remember that the right opportunity is out there for you. Relax, be patient, and as you continue your efforts, have confidence that you will find it.

Humanize the Organization

Try not to be intimidated by the organizational structure of a prospective customer. Instead, think of an organization like a living, breathing entity with needs and wants.

After all, businesses are operated by people just like you and me. Policies and job descriptions are put into place by these people and are modifiable according to the changing needs of those they serve.

For example, I may be told one day by someone, "We are not interested." However, it is entirely possible that the next day or month a department manager may have a sudden, pressing need for what you have. A "no" today does not necessarily mean a "no" tomorrow.

> *Recently I had to tell a sales candidate that the sales position I was hiring for was closed because we had filled the spot. Two weeks later the new employee unexpectedly left to take another job. Guess what? I called the alternate back and said he was back in the game.*

Treat a target company like the fickle entity that it is. Do not take any statement by someone as a written-in-stone fact. Many variables can influence a company in ways that are favorable to your purposes. Often, it is just a matter of having a conversation with the right person at the right time.

Humanize the Manager

There is a real person behind the desk and title. Like you, he is an individual with a distinctive personality. He is interested in meeting someone who can help him. If you can connect with him, you are more likely to get the response you desire.

> *I once helped a man recently released from jail. We worked together and he found a great job. The night before he was to begin, they called to cancel their offer because he had not been honest about his jail time on the application. The next morning, he and I went together to meet with the hiring manager and discuss the problem. An hour later, after we explained the situation and connected with him, the manager reconsidered his decision and reinstated him.*

Think of a prospective customer as someone with specific objectives to accomplish. As he evaluates candidates, he will probably consider the following:

- Will you bring the intended value to the organization and make him look good?
- Will your personality mesh or conflict with his as the supervisor?
- Will you share his goals and relieve some of his burdens?

Try to draw out these interests and concerns, and then relax and be yourself. If a connection forms, you may be on the path to success. If not, you'll try again somewhere else.

He Needs You as Much as You Need Him

It's easy to think of yourself as inferior compared to the others. But his business would not survive without people like you.

What would a CEO of a company do if he had no one to carry out his orders? Businesses spend billions of dollars per year recruiting, training, and retaining valuable employees.

By offering your services, you are actually doing him a favor, saving him time and money to find you. This becomes especially true as you gain higher levels of value and leverage.

Remember that he needs your product or service to run his business. You are a supplier of something valuable to his organization.

He needs you as much—or possibly more—than you need him. Your task is to find the company that will benefit the most from what you have to offer.

Peek Behind the Curtain

My first job out of undergraduate school was selling large commercial truck tires for a manufacturer. I was sent to Oregon to sell through six independent tire dealers, with an annual quota of twenty-thousand tires. I knew that these self-made business owners were not pushovers. I'd even been told they could be downright cantankerous, especially with a rookie.

One particular store owner was notorious for his foul disposition. Before my first meeting with him, I sat in my newly-issued company car reminding myself that he was just a person and that I could handle anything he dished out.

After we talked for a while, I noticed several pictures of a dog displayed on his office wall. I began asking him questions about the pictures. As he described the dog, to my surprise (and maybe to his), he started getting emotional, his eyes welling up with tears.

This customer—initially brusque and intimidating—transformed into an approachable person. I encouraged him to talk about something meaningful to him, and we were able to develop an amiable relationship.

In relationships, it is easy to be intimidated by titles and outward appearances. However, there is usually much more to the person than what you see on the outside. Look deeper, ask questions, and find the vulnerable person inside that you may be able to help.

Every man is a volume if you know how to read him.

—William Ellery Channing

Ride Out the Cycle

There are natural cycles to many aspects of life. We all experience seasons of success and prosperity, as well as seasons of stagnation, failure or disappointment.

Health, relationships, and finances ebb and flow from difficult to easy and back again, like the ocean's tide. Hopefully, as we go through these cycles, we learn from the challenges and opportunities they present.

> *My six-year-old son had been in the hospital for five weeks with some very serious neck and head surgery. My wife and I were exhausted and discouraged.*
>
> *One day, as we stepped into the hospital elevator for what seemed like the millionth time, we noticed a little piece of paper stuck to the wall that read, "In the end everything will be okay; if it's not okay, it's not the end."*

All cycles have an end. If you are currently in a down-cycle, be comforted in knowing that eventually things will go up again. Do everything you can to make your situation better and then ride out the difficult times with courage and patience.

Embrace the Struggle

Making changes, whether forced or voluntary, will probably lead to some painful experiences. No path is without some rejections, mistakes, and other disappointments.

Accepting the difficulties inherent in making changes can actually make things easier. By allowing stress and tension to be a part of the process, you are released from trying to over-control things. You will be free to take more risks and maximize the benefits of your experience in spite of the pain it causes.

At a certain point in my career one of my businesses failed, and I sold it for a loss. I was in debt, frustrated, and discouraged. However, the things I learned during that painful time have helped me in my subsequent business ventures.

Opportunities followed my failure which would not have otherwise presented themselves, including the writing of this book. Looking back, I am truly grateful for those difficult experiences.

You can choose whether to become embittered by adverse circumstances or strengthened and taught by them. Suffering and difficulties can be tools that transform you into a better, wiser person. Learn to accept and embrace the struggle.

What man actually needs is not a tensionless state, but rather the striving and struggling for some goal worthy of him. What he needs is not the discharge of tension at any cost, but the call of a potential meaning waiting to be fulfilled by him.

—Victor Frankl

See the Bigger Picture

Imagine yourself as a living house. God comes in to rebuild that house. At first, perhaps, you can understand what He is doing. He is getting the drains right and stopping the leaks in the roof and so on; you knew that those jobs needed doing and so you are not surprised. But presently He starts knocking the house about in a way that hurts abominably and does not seem to make any sense. What on earth is He up to?

The explanation is that He is building quite a different house from the one you thought of—throwing out a new wing here, putting on an extra floor there, running up towers, making courtyards. You thought you were being made into a decent little cottage; but He is building a palace. He intends to come and live in it Himself. –*C.S. Lewis*

Sometimes life twists and turns in ways that we do not expect and that are largely out of our control. We may have a change in our circumstances, like an illness, bankruptcy, or divorce. We may lose interest. We may feel like our goals are worthless, and our efforts at fulfillment are doomed to failure.

At crossroads like these, it may help to look at our lives from a very broad perspective. Perhaps the negative things that happen to us are the exact experiences that will help us to become better people.

By definition, these challenges are experiences through which we would not choose to go; and yet they contribute to our individual development dramatically. No matter what your faith or definition of God, a belief that your life challenges will contribute to your development and, ultimately, your happiness, can help you survive the difficult times.

Creative Expression

For a fortunate few, artistic talents naturally develop into paid work. For the rest of us, individual creativity is a more subtle component of success. As we discover a specific interest or talent in ourselves, we have the opportunity to use it creatively.

Incorporate creativity into your daily activities, whether paid or unpaid. As you express yourself in this way, your energy and passion for living will increase, you will feel happier, and the quality of your work may improve as well.

> *When I sold my business for a loss, I was at a low-point. Although I had no musical experience, I suddenly had an overwhelming urge to learn how to play the acoustic guitar. Over the next two years, I took lessons, performed in my first recital, and entertained my family with my limited skills.*
>
> *I experienced a therapeutic renewal of my perspective as I played. The guitar renewed my optimism in the future and in my ability to succeed.*

If you are having a hard time staying motivated or achieving your goals, it may be time to rediscover your artistic self. Find something that ignites your interest, absorb yourself in it, and share it with others. As you begin to enjoy creative experiences, you will be better able to pursue your ideal life.

Men are failures, not because they are stupid, but because they are not sufficiently impassioned.

—Maxwell Struthers Burt

Do Your Best and Heave the Rest

While pursuing your desired goals, remember that you are not in complete control of the outcome. At some point, after you have done everything you know to do, decide to have peace of mind, whatever the outcome may be. Choosing to let go of the things you cannot control relieves a lot of stress.

> *For a few years, I sold enterprise software in a very competitive environment. I spent a lot of energy worrying about what my competitor was doing and how my prospect felt about me versus him. One day, I decided to stop thinking about my competitor since his behavior was out of my control. Instead, I focused my attention on my relationship with the customer.*

Shifting my attention changed that job for me—primarily because I eliminated a huge amount of stress as I put my energy into meeting the needs of my customers.

The competitors to your success are the many variables which factor into outcomes over which you have little influence. Budget restrictions, others' qualifications, timing, and personality differences are just a few of these issues.

You can choose to worry about them, or you can focus your best efforts on the things that you can influence, and let go of the rest.

Don't Force It,
Let the Stars Align

As helpful as proactivity can be, there is a time to let circumstances naturally evolve. Remember, the goal is to find a mutually beneficial arrangement.

If you are too hasty and push yourself into a potential position, it may not end up benefiting you as much as you had hoped. It takes patience to search for the best fit.

There is no end to opportunities. Do not force a fit because you are feeling desperate or are tired of looking around. If the timing isn't right or the situation doesn't seem to make sense, move on.

If you are confident about your value and stay engaged in the process, you do not need to worry. When the right thing finally comes along, it will be a great opportunity on both sides. You will benefit from the experience and others will benefit from your abilities.

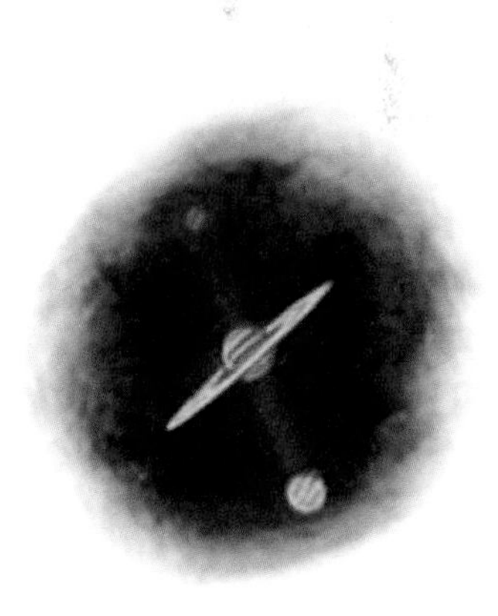

SMART – Test

Test, Learn, Adjust

Become a scientist by applying the scientific method. Remember, scientists start by asking a question. Then they test their assumptions with some kind of action, gather the resulting data, and determine if their hypothesis is correct. Should you not behave in a similar way?

Imagine, for example, that you are detail-oriented and proficient with numbers. You decide that you might enjoy being a bookkeeper or accountant. This is your hypothesis; now test it with action. You could get an entry-level bookkeeping job, take a couple of accounting classes or ask your current employer if they need any help in their accounting department.

Whatever option you try, you will get feedback that can assist you in deciding whether to continue on this career track or make adjustments. Your choices will be based on real experiences and not on your doubts or fears about yourself or the future.

In addition, objective evaluation of your progress will enable you to more precisely define what you want—your desires, goals, preferences, or aspirations—and have the motivation to pursue it.

I am always doing that which I cannot do in order that I may learn how to do it.

—Pablo Picasso

Assumptions in a Vacuum

One of the most notorious killers of momentum is what I call assumptions in a vacuum—a cycle of thinking that excludes taking action. It's like being stuck in a cave of thoughts and never venturing out into the real world.

These assumptions are usually positive or neutral. (We'll deal with the negative ones later.) The main characteristic of these thoughts is that they never lead to action. You endlessly think about ideas without doing anything.

Examples include:

- I could start a business.
- I could get paid more if I went back to school.
- I could go to the gym every day.
- I could work from home.
- I could stop wearing a tie to work.

Brainstorming is good. At some point, however, these ideas must be tested. If you stay too long in the idea stage and don't test your assumptions with actual experience, this thought pattern will inhibit your progress.

Instead of getting stuck in a "thought cave," use your great ideas as a springboard to decide what your goals will be and lay out a plan to achieve them.

Blanket Statements

Blanket statements are the negative cousins of assumptions in a vacuum. Unlike the brainstorming quality of those assumptions, these thoughts are dangerous generalizations that could stop you completely.

Blanket statements might include messages like:

- The economy is down.
- No one is hiring.
- Mondays are a bad time to call people.
- Fridays are a bad time to call people.
- No one's in the office at 5:00 p.m.

These types of discouraging statements are things you have probably heard from people who accept bad circumstances as unalterable facts. What happens when you test these ideas with action? Sometimes they are true, and sometimes not.

Do not let blanket statements stop you from making consistent efforts toward success. Unwrap yourself from their grasp by doing some research and making some calls.

Many of us have created lives that give very little support for experimentation. We believe that answers already exist out there, independent of us. What if we invested more time and attention to our own experimentation? We could focus our efforts on discovering solutions that work uniquely for us.

—Margaret Wheatley

Fool's Kryptonite

The messages of Fool's Kryptonite are more personal, negative assumptions that lead to stagnation. Like Superman, the kryptonite of self-doubting thoughts can overwhelm your self-confidence and paralyze your efforts to achieve your goals.

Some of these thoughts might be:

- I'm not smart enough.
- I'm not creative/musical/talented enough.
- I'm not attractive.
- I'm too old/young.
- I'm too fat/skinny/tall/short.
- I have ADD/other disabilities.
- I didn't go to college.
- I job-hopped too much/not enough.
- I got fired from my job.

For each thought of Fool's Kryptonite that threatens to hamper your progress, decide whether you ought to work through it (with books, journaling, therapy, etc.), or ignore it. Whatever defensive measures you take against these self-defeating thoughts, test them ruthlessly with action and real experience. Do not submit to them unconsciously and accept an unproven defeat.

Doubting Specter

Messages of inability, failure, unworthiness, or self-doubt may plague your thoughts. Perhaps they are self-created, a natural process of making a change or trying something new. Perhaps they sound like a critical parent, teacher, or not-so-supportive friend from your past. Whatever their origin, those thoughts can begin to sound like a voice in your head, a "doubting specter," that shadows your efforts at critical moments and stops you from making progress.

Craig had connected briefly with a potential investor for a museum-quality art project. Then his doubting specter took control. For two months Craig was discouraged and felt no confidence in himself or his idea. He discontinued his efforts to connect with the investor or develop his plans.

Finally, the investor called Craig back. It happened to be one of the first days that Craig had begun to feel confident again in his idea and abilities. He was able to overcome his thoughts of self-doubt and proceed with his project. They are now working together to make his idea a reality.

Craig's experience is not unique. Recognize when your doubting specter is overwhelming your confidence. Do not let it waste your time and frustrate your success by filling your mind with uncertainty. Learn to battle those thoughts by ignoring them and continuing with your plan of action. Focus on the process—making calls, going to appointments, meeting contacts—and you will succeed.

Our doubts are traitors, and make us lose the good we oft might win, by fearing to attempt.

—William Shakespeare

Creative Problem Solving

A respected Silicon Valley entrepreneur and investor said that after seeing many start-up businesses succeed or fail, the common denominator of success was the "relentless resourcefulness" of the managers in the successful companies.

The managers who continued to find new ways to solve the problems they encountered were more likely to succeed. Creativity and determination predicted their success in spite of very real challenges.

> *Anderson Cooper, the well-known CNN journalist, was having a hard time finding his first broadcasting job. He drew on his ingenuity and flew to Burma. Using his own equipment, he photographed and interviewed revolutionaries, sold his story to a network, and launched his successful career.*

Don't stop after hitting one, two, or three obstacles—that's usually when an optimal solution is near. Instead, take a step back and look at your situation from another angle. Think of specific questions you can ask yourself to help you creatively solve any issues that are currently problems for you.

Brainstorm new ideas, from logical to crazy, and jot them down or bounce them off a friend. Allow ideas to build upon themselves, leading to new and unexpected conclusions. You will be amazed at the results.

Imagination is more important than knowledge.

—Albert Einstein

Everything is Negotiable

Everything is negotiable. Well, almost everything. You should assume that you can negotiate anything until you have proof that you cannot.

Organizations create policies so that operations are not haphazard. When someone tells you that they cannot do something because it is against their policy, remember that policies were made by people.

They can be modified or broken by people as well. If you can connect with a reasonable manager, and show how the company can benefit by altering their procedure, you may get the change you want.

Here are some common policies that you could challenge:

- We don't take cold calls.
- We're not hiring.
- We have no budget.
- We don't pay more than $60K for that position.
- You must fill out an application before we can talk.

Employees, receptionists, and managers can sometimes become so obsessed with executing policy that they forget to interact with the individual. Help managers understand how you will be able to make their job easier. They may be willing to negotiate with you and adapt their policy in your favor.

Better to Ask Than to Wonder

It is better to ask for what you want and be denied than to wonder later whether you should have asked. If you feel the urge to ask for more money or for better terms, always do it; it might yield a huge return.

> *I had lunch with a client who was laid off from his company and was offered a generous severance package. A few days after receiving the paperwork, a colleague called and encouraged him to ask for more. He followed the tip and ended up with about $70,000 more than the original settlement.*

If you are tempted to assume that there is no leeway in the terms of a given opportunity, test that assumption by asking.

> *A couple of years ago, my brother and I rolled up to a hotel on two Harleys. The hotel attendant had seen our bikes as we rode up. I asked if she had a military discount. She said no. Then, stone-faced silence.*
>
> *I asked if she had any other discounts. She cheerfully informed us that there was a Harley discount we could use. Afterward I asked her if she would have offered the Harley discount had I not asked. She said she was trained to wait until someone brings it up.*

The world will wait for you to ask—so do it. Whatever the answer, yes or no, you will be more informed, you will have peace of mind, and you may benefit significantly in the process.

Always Counter Offer

When you receive an offer, there is almost always something else to negotiate if you are willing to ask for it. No matter how generous the offer seems, my rule is to always ask for more.

For example, if you were to receive an employment offer with a salary of $60,000, you might say, "Thank you for the offer, I really appreciate it. I think it would be great to work with you. Would you consider boosting the salary to $70,000?"

> *A company declined Brandon's counter offer for more salary, but granted his request for double the stock options if he met his first annual sales goal. He met the goal and they doubled his stock. A few years later the company went public and that request ended up being worth $190,000.*

There is almost always something on the table in a negotiation. In my experience, when you ask with confidence and conviction, you will usually get at least a little more.

> *Just this week, I was making an offer to a salesperson. He was happy with the compensation package, but asked for an extra five days of vacation time. Do you think he got it? He did.*

Make sure you don't leave anything on the table. Counter offer until the table is clean.

Everything you want is out there waiting for you to ask. Everything you want also wants you. But you have to take action to get it.

—Jules Renard

Conclusion

By having an autonomous agent mindset and applying the SMART Living concepts, you will be able to have more control and create a life that is customized to your goals. You will have more choices over what you do and how you do it.

The "magic bullet" in this process is taking action. Consistent activity will be the most important factor in your success. As you make direct contact, grow your value, connect with others, and test your assumptions, you will discover the life that you want.

It may seem intimidating to begin creating a custom-designed life. Hopefully, these ideas give you more confidence and energy to pursue your plan. If you are willing to put into action the suggestions given here, you will set yourself apart and feel more empowered to accomplish your goals.

Inaction breeds doubt and fear. Action breeds confidence and courage. If you want to conquer fear, do not sit home and think about it. Go out and get busy.

—Dale Carnegie

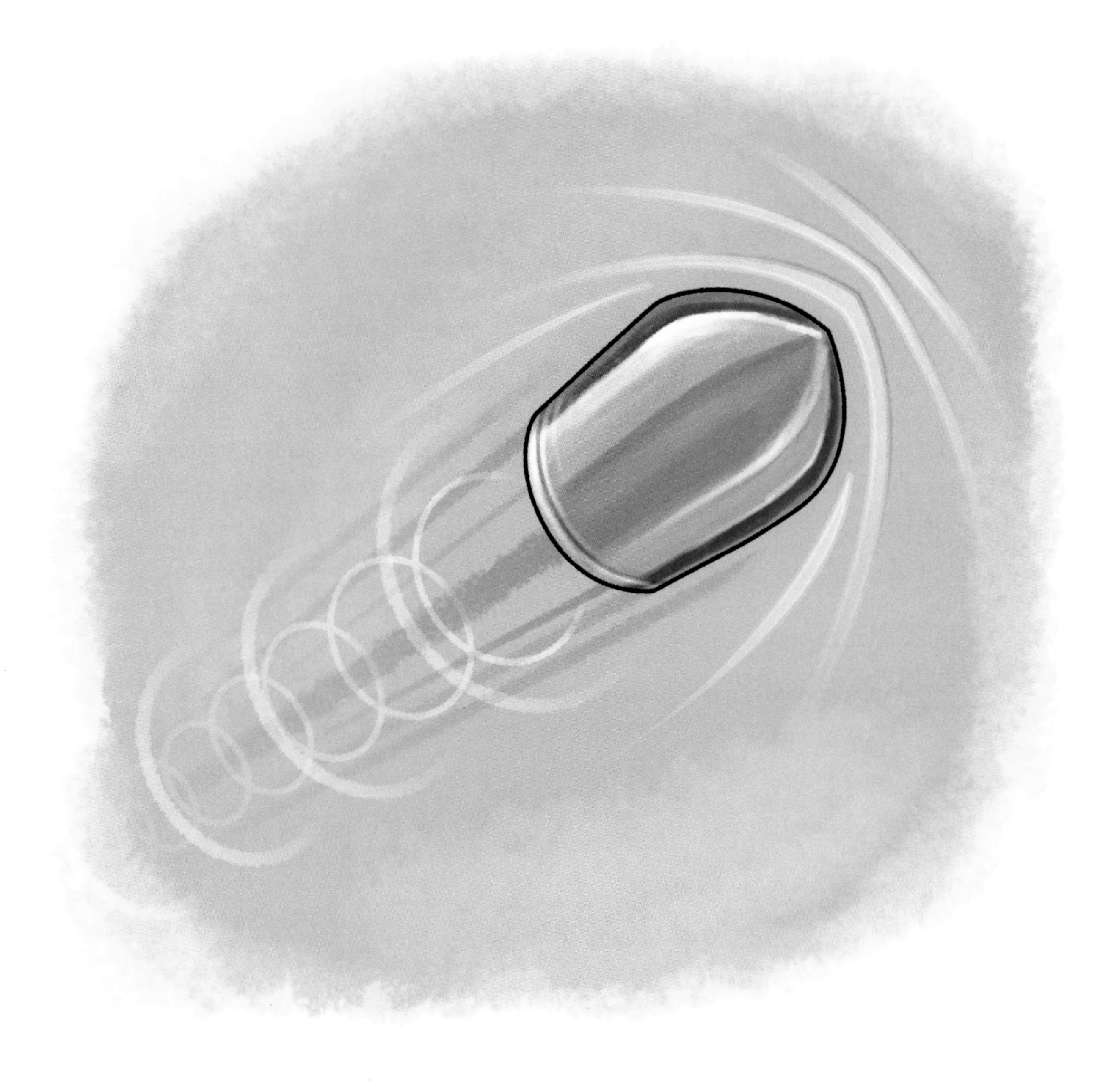

About the Author

Over the past eighteen years, John Boyd has been involved with over a dozen technology start-ups as a salesperson, manager, consultant, or founder. He is currently the President of J-Curve Sales, a Business-to-Business (B2B) Sales Outsourcing company.

John has used his experience to help many people achieve their goals and improve their lives. John also likes to play guitar, write songs, make movies, and do stand-up comedy. When he can, he likes to ride his dirt bike and go on cross-country Harley rides with his brothers.

He received a bachelor's degree in Business Management from Brigham Young University and an MBA from the University of Utah. He resides near Salt Lake City, Utah with his wife and seven children.

Visit John's website at *www.mjohnboyd.com* for more information about his sales outsourcing, speaking, and coaching services.

www.mjohnboyd.com